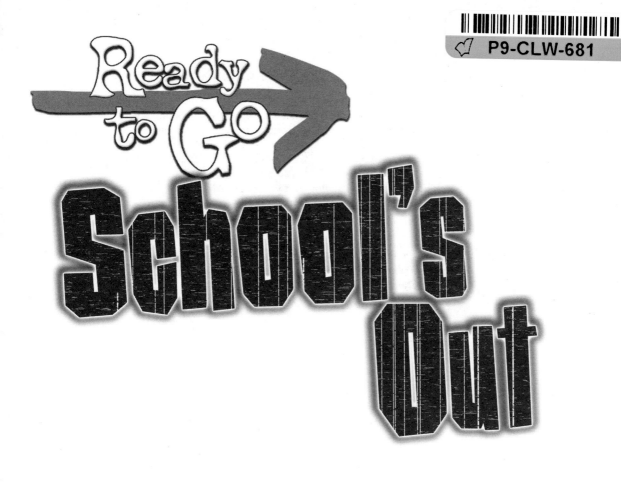

Ready to Go
School's Out

Youth Ministry
Ideas for
School Breaks
and Summer
Vacations

09 10 11 12 13 14 15 16 17 18– 10 9 8 7 6 5 4 3 2 1

MANUFACTURED IN THE UNITED STATES OF AMERICA

Editor: Josh Tinley
Design Manager: Keely Moore
Production Editor Supervisor: Sheila K. Hewitt

Designer: Keely Moore
Cover Design: Keely Moore

Dedication

To Calvary United Methodist Church

Contents

Introduction 8

The Long and Short of Summer Vacation 11

Starry-Eyed Wonders.................................12

Into the Deep 13

Dunk Tank 14

Happy Trails 15

Gardens for God 16

Going to the Fair 17

The Mall Haul 18

Church Camp, Anyone? 20

Cool Devotion 22

Prize-Winning Devotion 23

Celebrating Teachers Devotion 24

Road Patrol 26

School Gifts..27

Fantastic Fall Break 28

Labor for a Day 29

Labor of Love 30

Carnival Capers 32

Veterans Day Remembrance 34

Awesome Autumn 35

What's Love Got to Do With It? 36

Halftime 38

Thanksgiving on the Wing 40

Thanks-Living Breakfast 41

Thanks . . . In All Circumstances 42

Thanksgiving Psalm 44

Christmas Break 45

Fear Not! 46

Light It Up! 47

Christmas Retreat 48

Sweet Christmas 52

Blue Christmas 53

The Twelve Days of Christmas 54

Jingle All the Way 57

Paper Angels 58

Yule House or Mine? 59

Worthwhile Winter Breaks...60

   The New Year 61

   New Things 62

   And Justice for All...64

   Martin Luther King, Jr., Day 66

   Pass It On..68

   Snow Angels 69

   Snowballs...70

   Presidents' Day 71

Spectacular Spring Break...72

   Stepping Out 73

   God Be With You...74

   Spring Fling..75

   Spring Cleaning...76

   Remember Me 77

Youth Leader Breaks and Renewal Adventures.............80

   Soul Rest 81

   If Only I Had the Time 82

   Tough Questions 84

   Reflection..86

   Re-Creation 88

Photocopiable Handouts

   Spring Break Devotional 92

   Spring Cleaning Devotional 96

Introduction

For as long as there have been schools and school years, students have basked in the glory of recess—whether long or short. These breaks from the routine, from the grind of reading, writing, and arithmetic, have long made the hearts of students beat a little faster with the anticipation of freedom. The school break—even the thought of it—has also been a staple of student song and lore for centuries.

When I was a child, our mantra on the last day of school was:

School's out! School's out!
Teacher's let the monkeys out!

And during my early teenage years, Alice Cooper's hit song "School's Out (for Summer)" was a smash.

Even Ferris Bueller had to have a day off now and then.

Every youth leader has asked herself or himself, What happens when school is not in session? Will teenagers attend a church youth event?

School breaks and summer vacations present some of the most challenging opportunities for youth leaders. Families are out of town. Many youth simply want a break from the routine. And even the most fun church activities have a difficult time attracting crowds.

Most youth leaders understand that they must take a different approach during school breaks, try new ideas, or offer events that are out of the ordinary to gain the attention of busy teens. Other ministries take "down time" during these breaks. Still others try to use built-in school breaks as opportunities to do long-term planning and strategizing for the rest of the year. And often, youth leaders themselves can use these breaks as a time to refresh their souls.

Years ago, when I was a fledgling youth leader, I attempted to do youth ministry during school breaks much in the same way I did during the school year. The results were less than stellar. Many events were only marginally attended, and for other events no one showed.

Later, knowing that I wouldn't be able to use the same ministry model year round, I asked my youth what they would enjoy doing over their school breaks. Not all of their ideas were manageable. But we planned trips. We formed small groups. And I found ways to use these breaks as opportunities to connect with teens in more personal ways.

A break from school can also mean a break from the humdrum routine of youth ministry. A break from ministry-as-usual gives you a great chance to try out new ideas and develop new leaders. Teenagers who might not normally attend a youth meeting will sometimes attend a special event when school is out. And when teenagers aren't in school, you actually have opportunities for travel, overnight stay, and all-day outings that might not be available during the school year.

In the classic teen movie *Ferris Bueller's Day Off,* a high school senior, played by Matthew Broderick, decides to play hooky for the day. However, in order to orchestrate his day off, Ferris has to first convince his parents that he is ill. He also has to convince his best friend and his girlfriend to join him in the one-day vacation, all the while fleeing from the principal and his jealous older sister, who are hot on his trail. The movie offers a hilarious glimpse into the life of one teenager who just wants a break from school. But Ferris is after more than just a break. He craves excitement. He wants thrills. He's after learning of a different variety. His zest for life takes him through the city of Chicago (where his parents work) and back to the suburbs. By the end of the movie Ferris has learned more about his best friend, his girlfriend, his parents, and himself.

Like Ferris, most teenagers (and adults, for that matter) crave a break from the routine. People tend to become bored by routine. We tire of the commonplace. We grow stale in the work-a-day week of textbooks, lectures, and meetings. We seek something new, something that jostles our brain stems and awakens our senses.

For these reasons, school breaks offer some of the most enticing and exciting opportunities for ministry to teenagers. Be sure to take these breaks into consideration when you put together your youth ministry calendar.

As you consider summer vacation, for example, take time to schedule in opportunities for service and growth. Many youth leaders have discovered the power of mission work and long-term service during the summer months. But not all of these opportunities have to be planned by the youth leader. There are dozens of organizations that work directly with teens to provide top-flight ministry to others. Some of these opportunities are just a phone call or a mouse-click away.

Summer break also brings with it a host of church camps, athletic camps, and outdoor projects for youth. Many congregations also use teenagers to staff summer church activities for children, such as vacation Bible school. And don't overlook summer jobs—and the unique experiences these jobs offer teenagers—as a means of educating youth about the meaning of employment, financial planning, and stewardship.

Here you'll find ideas to use during the long summer vacation, as well as during shorter breaks such as Labor Day; Thanksgiving; Martin Luther King, Jr., Day; and Memorial Day. You'll even find some ideas for snow days. Try a few of these learning experiences, games, and outings and see if you can't spice up your school breaks and create a youth ministry experience your teenagers will enjoy and appreciate.

But don't overlook the fact that school breaks can also benefit youth leaders. Lest the busy youth leader think that this book is just about taking the job up another notch, working more hours, or foregoing vacation to spend more time with teenagers—don't despair. The final chapter of this book contains several rejuvenating suggestions about how to use a school break to revive the spirit, find much-needed rest, or pursue new learning. A school break can often be a perfect time to make time—time for yourself, your family, and your soul.

My hope is that this book will be a useful tool for the youth leader and the teenager alike.

School may be out, but your ministry to teenagers doesn't have to shut down when the school closes. God is always at work.

Ready to Go

The Long and Short of Summer Vacation

For most teenagers, summer vacation constitutes the longest and most rewarding break from school. These weeks in June, July, and August give teens some unique opportunities to enjoy outdoor activities and to participate in outings that can have a life-changing impact.

In many congregations, the youth group does a mission trip or the bulk of its outdoor fundraising (such as car washes) during the summer. Other churches hold youth rallies, summer camps, or outdoor concerts. Summer break can also be a time to consider some learning opportunities that fall outside the scope of your usual Sunday school, youth group, and Bible study offerings.

The hope is that you'll find two or three summer suggestions in this chapter that can make your youth ministry richer and fuller and that will provide meaningful, life-changing experiences for your youth.

STARRY-EYED WONDERS

Preparation: Find an observatory or amateur astronomer to host your group.

Supplies: Bible, a few flashlights

If you want to create an event that is both educational and fun, arrange for a high-quality stargazing event for your group. Many universities will open their observatories to groups if you call in advance. And many highly qualified buffs, with large, portable telescopes will be willing to set up an evening for your group for a small honorarium or on a volunteer basis.

Arrange for the expert to focus on some of the best and brightest stars in the night sky, giving commentary about each one and allowing time for questions and answers. If the moon is in the right phase, your group can also have fun looking at craters and other lunar surface features.

Bring a Bible and a few flashlights to this event.

Begin your devotional time together by reading aloud **Genesis 1:1-19.** Then ask:

➜ What does this story of creation tell us about the heavens?

➜ Which questions about the formation of the universe does this biblical account answer? Which questions does it not answer?

➜ What questions about the stars and the cosmos does this Scripture raise?

Read aloud **Psalm 19,** then ask:

➜ How do the stars reveal God's glory?

➜ What does the vastness of the universe tell you about God and creation?

➜ Does knowing that you live in a vast universe make you feel more intimately connected with God, or less so? Explain.

➜ How might looking at the stars increase our faith in God?

Close your stargazing experience by reading aloud **Psalm 8.**

INTO THE DEEP

Preparation: Locate and gather information for a nearby cave that is open to the public.

Supplies: Bible, flashlights, pens, pocket-size notebooks

Caving is a popular summertime excursion. A cave visit on a hot summer day will provide a cool place to visit and will provoke some lively discussion afterward. Check with the National Park Service or your state's department of natural resources to learn what nearby caves are open to the public.

During or after your caving adventure, talk about **1 Kings 19:4-18,** in which Elijah, on the run from Queen Jezebel, hid in a cave.

To begin, ask the youth to write in their notebook some of their impressions about the cave: sights, sounds, smells, feelings, and so forth. Ask:

➜ How would you describe the cave?

➜ What fears did being in the cave provoke?

➜ What kind of refuge or protection would a cave provide?

Read aloud **1 Kings 19:4-18,** then ask:

➜ Why was Elijah spending the night in a cave?

➜ How did Elijah experience God in the cave?

➜ What is significant about the way God chose to be revealed?

➜ How do light, air, and water play a part in our awareness of God?

➜ How might silence be important to a life of faith?

Close with a prayer thanking God for being present with us even in times of darkness.

THE DUNK TANK

Preparation: Secure a dunk tank; advertise the event.

Supplies: dunk tank, promotional materials

To have fun and raise money during the summer, have a dunk tank. You can usually rent these tanks from a party store. Line up several people in your congregation who are known for having a good sense of humor to sit in the tank. (Make sure that these people are willing to get wet for a good cause.)

Advertise the event well in advance, and let the community know whom it will have a chance to send falling into cold water. Have an enthusiastic person at the tank who can serve as a barker to invite passersby to "step right up" and try to hit the target. (Youth could take turns being the barker.)

You may also use the dunking booth in conjunction with another fundraising event, such as an ice cream social or a fish fry.

Important: A dunking booth is a large object with several moveable parts. Therefore, it requires adult supervision at all times.

HAPPY TRAILS

Preparation: Locate and gather information about a nearby hiking trail. Check with your local parks or recreation department to obtain a list of national, state, county, or city parks in your area that have hiking trails. Ask the parks in advance for trail maps.

Supplies: trail maps, copies of Scripture passages, pens, pocket-size notebooks, plenty of drinking water, food and other supplies for a cookout (optional)

Summer is a great time to take a youth group on a nature hike. Your group can take a simple hike, or you might choose to make a list of trees and wildlife that you'd like for the youth to identify during the outing. Have plenty of adult chaperones to help.

Trail hiking helps to form special bonds among teenagers. Consider beginning or ending the outing with a campfire cookout.

Before, during, or after the hike, your group might read and reflect on a Scripture that speaks of the beauty of creation (such as **Psalm 104**) or of getting away from the busyness of daily life (such as **Matthew 13:13-23**).

GARDENS FOR GOD

Preparation: Mark off garden plots on your church lawn (with your church leaders' permission). Be sure to secure access to water at the same time you obtain permission to use the church's land.

Supplies: Bible, tools to till the ground and to mark off garden plots, a convenient source of water

If your church has lawn space that is not being used, see whether church leaders would be willing to allow your group to set up a garden plot. The youth group can use wooden boards to outline 10-foot-by-10-foot garden plots. Leave walking room between the plots.

Across the country, in towns large and small, people are looking for garden plots to rent for the summer. Many people no longer have space in which to grow their own vegetables or flowers and would be willing to rent a garden plot for a few dollars. So the garden plot can help generate money for the youth group. If the goal isn't to raise money but to provide garden space as a mission project, provide rent-free garden plots to persons who might be open to this unique expression of love and care from the church.

Unused plots can be tended by the youth group for the summer and can be used to grow flowers for homebound persons or vegetables to donate to a food bank or raise money for a fundraiser. Your congregation probably has expert gardeners who would be willing to put their time and energy into this kind of endeavor.

As you prepare your garden project, you might study a relevant Scripture such as **Deuteronomy 24:19-22** ("Do not glean what is left [from your crops]; it shall be for the alien, the orphan, and the widow" [verse 21]). (See also **Exodus 23:10-11** and **Leviticus 19:9-10.**)

GOING TO THE FAIR

Preparation: Plan a trip to the fair, and prepare a scavenger hunt list.

Supplies: scavenger hunt lists, plastic grocery bags to carry the bulkier finds, small plastic bags to carry small items in

The summer months mean county fairs and state fairs. Many youth have never been in a fair environment and are quite taken with the sights, sounds, and smells of this unique summer experience, which can help group members form some new bonds with one another.

If you are looking to create a fun experience at the fair, try this unusual scavenger hunt game. Divide the group into teams, and give each team some plastic bags and the following list of items that they must find at the fair.

Feel free to add to or change this list. Also decide ahead of time whether teams may earn points for finding more than one of a particular item. For example, if the youth find 2 soft drink cans, will they earn 2 points or just 1? Consider too the time it might take to count, for example, 359 pieces of straw.

1-point items

→ Candy wrapper

→ Ice cream stick

→ Corn dog stick

→ Soft drink can

→ Paper cup

→ Napkin

→ Packet of ketchup or mustard

→ Packet of sugar

→ Coffee stirrer

5-point items

→ Sawdust (about 1 teaspoonful)

→ Bird feather

→ Piece of straw

→ Ear of corn

→ Pie

10-point items

→ Ticket stub

→ Badge

→ Unmelted ice cube

→ Sunglasses

→ Umbrella

→ Whistle

THE MALL HAUL

Another fun summertime destination is the mall. Here are some fun summer games that you can do at the local shopping mall.

THE DOLLAR CHALLENGE

Supplies: Bible, one dollar for every few youth

Divide the group into teams, and give each team a dollar. Specify a time limit and a meeting place. See which team can purchase the most items with its dollar. After the groups have purchased their items, challenge them to think of ways to put them to use. (For example, if they were to purchase plastic bug rings, bouncy balls, and toy whistles, they might decide to give these samll items to the children in the congregation.) Follow this up, if you would like, with a devotion on stewardship of what God has given us. Consider using **Matthew 25:14-30** (the parable of the talents) or **Mark 6:30-44** (the feeding of the 5,000) as a key text. Both of these Scriptures are about getting the most out of what God has given us, even if what God has given us seems meager.

PROGRESSIVE DINNER

Go to the mall food court and have a progressive dinner, eating appetizers at one place, main course at another, and dessert at a third. Add another fun element (and good stewardship) to the mix by setting a spending limit.

18

THINKING OF YOU

Supplies: one dollar for each youth

Give each teen a dollar, and invite everyone in the group to purchase a small item that can be given to a friend along with an invitation to attend youth group meetings and events. This is a fun and simple means of evangelism that can help your group grow and to minister to new members.

MOVIE AND MEANING

Most malls have a cinema inside or nearby. Watch a movie together. Afterward, discuss the film, using questions such as:

➔ With which character did you most identify? Why?

➔ What Christian themes (such as love, grace, and redemption) were at play in this story?

➔ What positive lessons can you take from this movie?

CHURCH CAMP, ANYONE?

Preparation: Gather church camp flyers and other supplies (see the list). Fill a small suitcase with the flyers.

Supplies: Bible, church camp flyers, suitcase, firewood and kindling, a means of lighting a fire (optional if you have a safe place to have a campfire), a means to extinguish a fire (necessary only if you plan to have a campfire)

Summer provides ample opportunity for youth to go to church camp. If you are looking to stir up some excitement for the camping opportunities in your area, give this interactive devotional a try. This devotional is best used before the end of school or at the beginning of summer vacation and is best held outdoors.

Before the meeting, stack the firewood on the ground as you would set up a campfire. Set aside one piece of kindling for each youth. When the youth arrive, ask them to gather around the unlit fire and spend some time thinking about their summer vacation plans. Pass the suitcase around the circle. Have each teen, when he or she has the suitcase, offer a brief explanation of his or her summer plans. These plans might include vacations, family outings, or work opportunities.

Once the suitcase has completed the circuit, read aloud **Ecclesiastes 5:18:** "This is what I have seen to be good: it is fitting to eat and drink and find enjoyment in all the toil with which one toils under the sun the few days of the life God gives us."

Ask:

➔ Why is relaxation important in our summer plans?

➔ Why are enjoyment and relaxation important to our spiritual growth and learning about God?

➔ Are you planning on or considering attending a church camp?

Following this brief discussion, give each youth a piece of kindling.

Say: "Perhaps some of you have considered going to church camp this year. Church camp is a wonderful opportunity to bond with other Christian teenagers and to grow in your faith. If you have considered going to church camp this year, please go to the suitcase and take out one of the flyers. These flyers contain the dates of the summer camps in our

20

area. If you will commit to going to camp, I ask that you place your kindling on the firewood as a sign of your commitment. The fire inside our circle remains unlit; but when you get to camp, you will find that there is a new fire that God will kindle in your life." Close in prayer.

If you are looking for creative ways to encourage your teenagers to attend church camp, consider one of the following options:

SUMMER CAMP POSTCARD

Preparation: Gather addresses of church camps that your youth will be attending.

Supplies: postcards, stamps

If you are looking for a quick way to stay in touch with your youth who attend summer camp, send out camp postcards. Most camps have post office boxes that will handle mail sent to campers.

Your postcard might include greetings from others in the church youth group, a message from you, and/or a few pertinent and encouraging Scripture verses.

LETTER TO MYSELF

Supplies: envelopes, stamps

Before a teen leaves for camp, give her or him a stamped envelope. Invite her or him to write a letter to herself or himself during his or her time at camp, reflecting on what she or he has learned and experienced and what commitments she or he has made. Tell the youth to mail the letter from camp to her or his home address.

COOL DEVOTION

Preparation: Prepare a bowl of assorted fruit chunks, trying to get the chunks about the same size and shape. (Be sure you know about any fruit allergies your youth might have.)

Supplies: Bible, blindfold, food service gloves (or plastic, food storage bags), bowl of assorted fruit chunks

Ask a volunteer to put on one food service glove or to put a plastic bag over one of his or her hands. Blindfold the volunteer and ask him or her to reach into the bowl and pull out a piece of fruit. Instruct the volunteer to taste the fruit and attempt to identify, based on taste alone, the type of fruit. (To take away the volunteer's sense of smell, which would help him or her identify the fruit, have the volunteer use the unbagged hand to hold his or her nose before choosing the fruit and while eating it.) You may choose to repeat this with other volunteers.

Then ask:

➜ Why is it easy or difficult to identify a piece of fruit from the taste alone?

➜ What other attributes might help you identify a piece of fruit?

Following these questions, invite another volunteer to read aloud **Galatians 5:22-25** (the fruit of the Spirit). Then ask:

➜ What is the apostle Paul talking about when he refers to the "fruit of the Spirit"?

➜ What "fruits" does Paul mention?

➜ How are these fruits related to one another?

➜ In what ways might these fruits of the Spirit help sweeten our lives or make us more productive in our faith?

➜ How easy or difficult is it to identify fruits of the Spirit in other Christians? Explain.

Allow the group to enjoy the fruit chunks. Close by asking someone to again read aloud **Galatians 5:22-23.**

PRIZE-WINNING DEVOTION

Preparation: Acquire a trophy or trophies.

Supplies: Bible, one trophy for one person or a small trophy for each person in the group

For this summer devotion, you'll need a Bible and one small trophy (or a small trophy for each person in the group).

Begin by asking each person in the group to describe a personal achievement that was particularly satisfying. Pass the small trophy around the circle and have each person, when he or she is holding the trophy, tell the group about his or her achievement. Or give a trophy to each person as he or she tells the group about an achievement. Make sure that everyone participates in this portion of the devotion.

Then ask:

➜ Why are goals important?

➜ Why, do you think, does achieving or reaching a goal feel so satisfying?

➜ What type of goals are most difficult to achieve?

Read aloud **Philippians 3:10-16.** Then ask:

➜ What words does the apostle Paul use here to describe the difficulty of obtaining the goal? (*press on, forgetting the past, straining forward, and so forth*)

➜ What is the goal that Paul is referring to here? (*the resurrection from the dead, salvation—see verse 11*)

➜ Why, do you think, did Paul describe this goal in athletic terms?

➜ Where or to whom can we look for help as we press on to achieve this ultimate goal?

Close by asking members of the group to tell their prayer concerns or other insights about the Philippians passage.

CELEBRATING TEACHERS DEVOTION

Preparation: Gather a small supply of back-to-school items.

Supplies: Bible, index cards, pens or pencils, back-to-school items to distribute to the youth group

This is a great devotion to use near the end of the summer break, as students are ready to begin another school year.

Begin by asking each student to write on an index card the name of a favorite teacher, along with a few bullet points that describe why this teacher is effective or well liked. Invite the youth to discuss their favorite teachers with the group. Then ask:

➜ Why are teachers important to us?

➜ What, in your estimation, makes a good teacher? What makes a good teacher exceptional?

Then say: "Let's hear a story about another famous teacher in the Bible. It may surprise you to learn that the apostle Paul studied with a very famous rabbi."

Read aloud **Acts 22:1-10.** Then ask:

➜ Why, do you think, did Paul mention his teacher, Gamaliel, when he was telling the story of his faith?

➜ What, do you imagine, did Paul learn from Gamaliel? What, do you think, did he learn from Jesus?

➜ In what ways do we look to Jesus as our teacher? What can we learn from him?

➜ Why is it important for us to learn from others about our faith?

Following this discussion time, ask the students to make a commitment to have a great year at school and to learn as much as they can from their teachers. Hand out the school supplies and close by reading aloud **Proverbs 8:10-11.** Then pray aloud the following prayer:

Gracious God, guard our hearts as we learn what is true and right. Help us have open minds and willing spirits as we go to school to learn more about our world and our place in it. Let us thank those who teach us; and let us look to Jesus, who has taught us all good things, that we might grow more and more each day into the likeness of his love. Amen.

ROAD PATROL

Preparation: Adopt a stretch road.

Supplies: Bible, supplies for cleaning up and beautifying your stretch of road

For a meaningful summertime service project, go on road patrol. There are many towns where a youth group can adopt a mile of highway or a strip of median. The group could not only pick up trash along this stretch of road but also plant flowers and find other ways beautify the area.

Use the quick devotional below to give your road patrol experience some depth.

Begin by reading aloud one or more of the following Scriptures:

➜ **Luke 10:29-37** (Jesus tells the parable of the good Samaritan on the road to Jericho.)

➜ **John 9:1-12** (Jesus heals a blind man on the side of the road.)

➜ **Acts 8:26-38** (Philip meets an Ethiopian official on the road and teaches him about Christ.)

Then ask:

➜ What significant act took place along the road in this story (or in these stories)?

➜ What sorts of things, do you think, do people think about as they drive down this road?

➜ What needs might people see as they drive down this road?

➜ What needs might they ignore or fail to notice?

➜ How might our work along the roadside be a witness to God's presence and care?

➜ What impact might our work have on the people who drive this stretch of road?

26

SCHOOL GIFTS

Preparation: Gather advertisements for back-to-school items.

Supplies: Bible, advertisements for back-to-school items, index cards, pens or pencils

This lesson can be used as a back-to-school devotion or as a Labor Day weekend experience that will help get teenagers ready to work.

As the teenagers arrive, give each person a section of the ads in the newspaper. Invite the youth to look through these ads and make a list of advertised items that he or she might need for school.

Then ask:

➜ What kinds of "tools" did you find in the ads that would be useful during your school year? How would you use these tools?

➜ Aside from things you can buy in a store, what other tools and gifts can you use that will help you have a good year at school?

Ask a volunteer to read aloud **1 Corinthians 12:1-11,** in which Paul discusses spiritual gifts. (You might choose to have several volunteers each read a verse or two at a time.) Give the teens a moment to reflect on the spiritual gifts that God has given them. Then ask:

➜ What are some of the spiritual gifts, or tools, that God has given you?

➜ How can you put these tools to work at school in the coming year?

Close by saying a prayer for the new school year.

Fantastic Fall Break

Most schools have some type of fall break and also honor autumn holidays such as Labor Day and Thanksgiving. The fall season usually lends itself well to outdoor activities, since the hot days of summer have passed. Depending on what part of the country you live in, you may witness the amazing color that comes with the change of season. As you make your plans for out-of-school days in the fall, try a few of these ideas and see if they don't spark some seasonal enthusiasm.

LABOR FOR A DAY

Preparation: Plan a Labor Day work project that meets a need in your community.

If you are looking for a hands-on Labor Day event, try using this school break as a time for your youth to give back to the community. There are several ways to do this.

→ Use Labor Day morning to work with youth around the church building—cleaning the yard, planting fall flowers, washing windows. Work with the trustees to create a list of projects the youth could accomplish in two or three hours.

→ Create a list of people in your community who need a helping hand, then have your youth take action. Recipients of your group's assistance might include older adults who need help around the house, in the yard, or with grocery shopping. Or your group might choose to volunteer in an assisted-living community.

→ Spend the weekend with the youth picking up trash in a town park or cemetery. Afterward, recycle as much of the trash as possible.

Fantastic Fall Break

READY-TO-GO SCHOOL'S OUT

LABOR OF LOVE

Preparation: Invite several guests to speak about their careers.

This Labor Day weekend event has always been well-received by youth—especially by those older teens who are considering a career or college major.

Make a list of 6–12 people in your congregation or community who have interesting careers. These might include people who are in the medical field, lawyers, people who own their own business, insurance representatives, beauticians, counselors, teachers, mechanics, and anyone else you think could talk intelligently and openly about the work that he or she does and what that work requires.

Invite these persons to your church one day during Labor Day weekend, and allow them to speak the group about their careers and their families. Arrange for these people to bring in tools of their trade, brochures, or other items that would give teens a better idea of what the career entails and where the teens might go for more information.

Also ask the invited guests to prepare answers to the following questions:

➔ Why did you enter your career?

➔ What are the requirements, educational and otherwise, for this career?

➔ What are the rewards and challenges of your work?

➔ What should teenagers consider in pursuing this career choice?

➔ What advice would you offer to teenagers today who are considering vocations?

Allow time for the youth to ask their own questions and for your career guests to talk with individual teenagers who may have particular interests.

Close with a prayer for guidance.

CARNIVAL CAPERS

Many communities have fall carnivals. Taking your group to a carnival environment is a wonderful way to not only have fun together but also to explore some of the party themes in Jesus' parables. Here are two workable ideas that can turn a fall carnival into a bonding event or a learning excursion.

PRIZE WINNERS

Preparation: Buy or create some simple prizes.

Supplies: Bible

Try this prize-winning game at the carnival. Hand out prizes to teens who win the following events:

→ The one who rides the most rides.

→ The one who eats the largest elephant ear (or funnel cake or other carnival desert of your choosing).

→ An additional prize to anyone to wins a stuffed animal (or the most stuffed animals).

→ A prize to the boy who scores the highest in a game (ring toss, skee ball, and so forth)

→ A prize to the girl who scores the highest in a game.

→ A prize to the teen who picks up the most trash.

→ A prize to the teen who recycles the most trash.

THE PARTY JESUS

Supplies: Bible

Before or after your visit to the carnival, engage the youth in this brief Bible study of two parables.

Read aloud **Luke 14:7-14,** then ask:

➜ What are some of the elements of the kingdom of God that Jesus describes in these parables?

➜ In what ways is the kingdom of God like a big party?

➜ Why, do you think, did Jesus often use a banquet or party atmosphere to describe God's work?

Read aloud **Luke 15:8-10,** then ask:

➜ How does this parable relate a sense of joy?

➜ Why, do you think, did the woman in the parable invite her friends to celebrate with her? Why didn't she keep the joy to herself?

➜ How might we be like the lost coin in this story?

➜ How might we be like the woman in this story?

➜ How is the celebration in this story like the kingdom of God?

VETERANS DAY REMEMBRANCE

Supplies: Bible, sword, shovel

Not all schools have a recess on Veterans Day. However, if your students' schools do, here is a brief morning study that can be used to give your teenagers a deeper appreciation for those who have served the nation.

Show the group a sword and a shovel. Invite one of the teenagers to read aloud **Isaiah 2:2-5.** Then ask:

➜ What is the vision of the prophet Isaiah?

➜ What is the kind of peace the prophet is speaking about?

➜ According to the prophet, how will true peace be accomplished?

➜ Why do people still long for peace today?

➜ Why might the soldier in the field want peace more than anyone else might?

You can make this study all the more powerful by gathering at a veteran's memorial or other marker in your community.

AWESOME AUTUMN

Preparation: Identify a tree-filled location where your group can observe the fall foliage.

Supplies: Bible(s), digital camera(s)

This outdoor meditation is perfect for colorful fall days. Take your group to a tree-filled location (a park, a farm, or a lookout point, for example) where you can observe the fall foliage.

Once you arrive at your location, allow each teenager to take several photos of the foliage. See who can take the most alluring and colorful photo. (Most digital cameras allow you to review the photos immediately on a display screen.) After you have reviewed these photographs, ask:

➔ What emotions do you attach to the fall season?

➔ What is most remarkable about this season?

Follow this brief discussion with a reading of **Psalm 104.** You might choose to have your youth read the Scripture, each person reading a verse at a time. As the Scripture is read aloud, ask the students to listen for specific imagery that the psalm evokes. Then ask:

➔ In what ways might this be considered a psalm of praise?

➔ What are some of the images from nature that the Psalm writer uses to demonstrate the majesty of God?

➔ How do you see good and evil at play in this psalm?

➔ If you were to write a psalm inspired by the glory of God's work on this day, what images and ideas might you include?

Close with a prayer of thanksgiving, or ask the teens to offer up individual prayers of thanks.

WHAT'S LOVE GOT TO DO WITH IT?

Preparation: Find a location where your group will have some degree of solitude. Enlist several adult volunteers.

Supplies: Bible, writing pad, and pen or pencil for each participant

This fall break event will get the youth talking about sexuality and communication. For the event, secure a private room in a restaurant or go to a park or other area that has some degree of solitude. Bring along other adult chaperones for this one, as most adults want to have plenty of support when discussing with teenagers issues of sex.

Gather your group together, and invite the teenagers to discuss the following opening questions:

➔ Why, do you think, is sexuality difficult to discuss?

➔ In what ways is communication important to a relationship?

➔ What, do you think, are some of the barriers to effective communication?

Invite three or four of the teenagers to read aloud the following passages from **The Song of Solomon: 1:1-3; 2:16-27; 4:1-5; 5:6-8.** Then ask:

→ How might poetry help us express our feelings for those we love?

→ What are some of the images and ideas that the man and woman in this Scripture use to express love for each other?

→ How is their communication helpful in expressing their love?

→ In what ways does love complicate a relationship? In what ways does love make a relationship less complicated?

As time allows, invite the young men and young women to meet apart from each other. Allow the two groups to ask questions about relationships, dating, sex, and so forth. Ask your chaperones to help the teenagers discuss these questions in an open and appropriate way.

Close with a prayer in the groups.

HALFTIME

Preparation: Get access to a locker room or private area at a recreational center and book a sports-related speaker.

Supplies: Bible

If you are looking for an activity to get your teenagers recharged for school, try this idea that can be used during a fall break or Christmas break. A locker room or a private area at a recreational center is a preferred setting for this activity.

You'll also need a coach, a pro or college athlete, or someone else who is involved in athletics to give you a hand with this one. Over the years, I've found that high school and college coaches are very amenable to this activity; and it has been a favorite and inspiring activity among the youth.

Upon arriving at your location, invite everyone to take a seat around the locker room. Begin by discussing one or two of the following questions:

➜ What is your favorite sport? Why?

➜ What makes this sport demanding or challenging?

➜ What special tools are needed to participate in this sport?

➜ What would happen if a person attempted to compete in this sport without the proper equipment?

➜ What about athletics inspires you?

➜ Why, do you think, do many people get away from participating in athletics when they get older?

➜ What, do you think, would keep someone "in the game" for a longer period of life?

Once you've had a chance to discuss a few of these issues and the youth have expressed their opinions, invite your guest coach or athlete to address the group. (Here it would be best to ask the coach to discuss how he or she inspires the team, particularly at halftime, when there is more game left to be played.)

After the coach has spoken, read aloud **Ecclesiastes 11:8–12:8.** Then ask:

➜ Why is it important for us to remember God in our youth?

➜ Why are our educational efforts important to our future? to God?

➜ What would inspire you to make the most of your education and the other opportunities that you have as a young person?

THANKSGIVING ON THE WING

Preparation: Find an opportunity to help serve meals on Thanksgiving, or host a Thanksgiving meal at your church.

Thanksgiving is one of the best service opportunities for youth. Many shelters, churches, and agencies welcome extra help serving Thanksgiving meals to needy persons. In fact, Thanksgiving is one of the few days during the year when many people will spend a morning helping others or giving back to the community.

Plan to take your teenagers on a hands-on service project at a shelter in your area; or if possible, have your teenagers help serve a Thanksgiving meal at your church that is open to the community. You'll be surprised at how many people attend and how much your teenagers will grow in their care for and service to others.

THANKS-LIVING BREAKFAST

Preparation: Prepare a copy of the list below for each person.

While most families will have a traditional thanksgiving lunch or dinner together later in the day, Thanksgiving morning can be an open invitation for the youth to gather. Plan a simple Thanksgiving breakfast centered around light fare and some moments of reflection. (If you'd like, ask the youth to pitch in various items for this breakfast.)

Use the list below to provoke some thankful reflections. Consider providing a copy of this list for each teen.

➔ The person who has influenced me most this year is _____

_____.

➔ The most wonderful thing that has happened to me this year is _____

_____.

➔ I have been most aware of God this year when _____

_____.

➔ My best memory this year is _____

_____.

➔ The most helpful thing I have learned this year is _____

_____.

➔ The best lesson I have learned this year is _____

_____.

➔ My greatest personal achievement has been _____

_____.

➔ I am most thankful for_____

_____.

➔ My faith has grown this year because_____

_____.

THANKS . . . IN ALL CIRCUMSTANCES

Supplies: Bibles, paper and pens or pencils for taking notes

If you have a venue in which to conduct a more in-depth Bible study with teens during the Thanksgiving break, try this study of the **Book of Philippians.** Gather the group, and begin by giving the following background:

> One of the most uplifting books of the Bible is Philippians. This is a letter to the church at Philippi, which Paul wrote when he was in prison. The tone of this letter is surprising, considering that Paul is no longer free and is uncertain of his future. Yet he wrote of things inspiring and of his faith in God.

> Often, when we experience hard times, we turn away from God. But difficulties can also draw us closer to God. These hardships can teach us that God is able to deliver us.

Divide the group into four teams (one team per chapter), and ask each team to read its respective chapter of Philippians and to make notes of the uplifting verses or themes that they find.

In the event that the youth miss the highlights, here are four verses (one from each chapter) that you can draw out for discussion:

Chapter 1: "I will continue to rejoice, for I know that through your prayers and the help of the Spirit of Jesus Christ this will turn out for my deliverance" (**1:18-19**).

Chapter 2: "Let each of you look not to your own interests, but to the interests of others" (**2:4**).

Chapter 3: "I press on toward the goal for the prize of the heavenly call of God in Christ Jesus" (**3:14**).

Chapter 4: "Rejoice in the Lord always; again I will say, Rejoice" (**4:4**).

Discuss the following questions, or provide them for small group reflection:

➜ Why, do you think, do hard times often strengthen our faith?

➜ How does prayer help during tough times?

➜ How do our difficulties relate to the suffering and sacrifice of Jesus?

➜ What can help us press on toward the heavenly prize?

➜ Why, do you think, is rejoicing important to our faith?

➜ What verse in Philippians could you memorize to help you through a tough time?

Close by praying together **Philippians 4:8.**

THANKSGIVING PSALM

Preparation: Prepare a handout or an e-mail for your youth.

If you have a busy youth group at Thanksgiving but want to give your teenagers a reflection tool to help in their family gathering, give each youth a sheet of paper or an e-mail containing the instructions and questions below:

Read aloud **Psalm 150** at your family gathering. Then ask:

→ How has our family been blessed this year?

→ What gifts has God given us?

→ For what are we thankful?

→ In what ways do we need God's help?

→ For what would we ask God today in our prayers?

Ready to Go →

Christmas Break

Perhaps no other school break offers as many possibilities for ministry as the lengthy respite from the rigors of schoolwork surrounding Christmas. Many teens find meaning in the traditions of decorating the tree, baking cookies, and hanging mistletoe at home. Others look forward to going Christmas caroling with the youth group, serving meals to persons and families in need, and attending candlelight church services.

The Christmas break is also one of the most compelling times for youth to invite friends and seekers to youth group gatherings and events. The possibilities for ministry during this season are tremendous.

As you consider the events, activities, and studies in this section, give consideration to the kind of experience you want your teenagers to have. Do they need a deeper awareness of God amid the trappings of the season? Do they need more awareness of the diversity of the world, a deepening heart for the poor and needy? Do they need more unity as a group?

It is hoped that you'll be able to find some compelling events here that will help you answer these and other questions. And may the blessings of the season fill your teenagers with peace and joy!

FEAR NOT!

Supplies: Bibles, index cards or small pieces of paper, pens or pencils

Hand out the cards and pencils, and ask someone in the group to read aloud **Luke 1:30-31.** Emphasize the words: "Then the angel said to Mary, 'Fear not!'" (KJV).

Say: "This phrase, 'fear not!' (or similar words of comfort, such as 'do not be afraid') appears frequently in the Bible. It is God's way of dispelling our fears when we are uncertain, when something unexpected happens and takes us out of the normal flow of life."

Ask the youth to write on the cards some of their greatest fears. These fears should be a bit deeper than a fear of spiders, snakes, or heights. Rather, what are the real fears that affect their daily lives?

After a few minutes, ask the following questions:

➜ How are fear and faith related?

➜ Why, do you think, is talking about our fears often so difficult?

➜ What happens when we confront our fears and talk openly about them?

➜ How does the assurance of God's presence displace or ease our fears?

➜ How has your faith in God helped you get through fearful experiences?

Close with a group prayer or by praying aloud and together **Psalm 23.**

LIGHT IT UP!

Preparation: Identify a room that can be completely darkened. String up some Christmas lights in the room, and have them ready to turn on.

Supplies: Bible, Christmas lights and a means to hang them up, flashlight

For this brief experiential meeting (or devotion), bring the group into the room. Once everyone is settled, turn out the lights so that the room is very dark.

Let everyone's eyes adjust to the darkness. Then ask a few youth to respond to the question, How would you describe darkness?

After some time for discussion and reflection in the dark, turn on the Christmas lights and read aloud **Isaiah 60:1.** Use the flashlight if needed.

Then ask:

➜ In what way is light necessary for us to have life (both literally and figuratively)?

➜ Are you more comfortable in light or darkness? Why?

➜ Why, do you think, did the prophets often use light as a metaphor for God?

➜ Why, do you think, did Jesus describe himself as the "light of the world" (**John 8:12**)?

Close this experience, if you choose to, by singing a few Christmas carols.

CHRISTMAS RETREAT

Preparation: Identify a setting for this retreat and gather the necessary supplies.

Supplies: Bibles, pens or pencils, paper, cookies, one small sprig of evergreen for each youth

The Christmas break is a perfect time to have a one-day youth retreat. Here are four modules that can be used as an afternoon retreat or an overnight event. The modules may be spaced out during the retreat and interspersed with games, silence, meals, and free time to create a full afternoon or evening.

MODULE 1: HOW BEAUTIFUL UPON THE MOUNTAINS

Give each youth a piece of paper and a pencil or pen, and have the youth find a partner for this brief study of **Isaiah 52:7-10.** Ask the pairs to read this passage together and then to discuss the following questions:

➜ What are some beautiful messages we hear today?

➜ Why do we crave good news?

➜ Why is God's salvation good news?

➜ How has God comforted you in the past year?

➜ What do you think of the prophet's vision that all the nations of the earth shall see the salvation of God?

➜ How does the anticipation of Christmas remind us of God's salvation?

After a few minutes, give each youth an evergreen sprig; and invite everyone to smell the aroma of his or her sprig. (The youth might have to pull off part of the sprig to smell it well.)

Ask the youth to write down three things they have experienced as good news in the past year and then to write three things they anticipate or hope that God will do for them in the coming year. Close with a group prayer.

MODULE 2: O TASTE AND SEE

For this module, ask the teens to get into groups of four to five. Give each group a plate of cookies. As the youth enjoy the cookies, invite them to discuss the following two questions:

• How do our senses (taste, smell, touch, and so forth) influence our experience of God?

• In what ways might we taste God's goodness?

After a few minutes, invite each group to read aloud **Psalm 34:8.** Ask the groups to discuss the following questions:

• Where have you seen God's goodness at work in our group?

• What experiences have we had as a group that have strengthened your faith?

Close this module in prayer.

MODULE 3: THE SAVIOR'S BIRTH

This module of the retreat will give youth the opportunity to explore Luke's nativity story more fully. Have the teens pair off and ask each pair to read the nativity story together (**Luke 2:1-20**).

Following the reading, ask the pairs to write down one question that they have about the Jesus' birth. With these questions in hand, reconvene as a large group and discuss the concerns, insights, or ideas that the youth have expressed. Allow plenty of time and don't be afraid of deep questions that may not have an easy answer or may lead to more questions.

Close this module by praying together the Lord's Prayer.

MODULE 4: GIFTS FOR THE KING

Ask the youth to break into comfortable groups of various sizes. (If you fear that groups will form based on cliques, you may choose to assign the groups yourself.) Invite the groups to read **Matthew 2:1-12** together and then discuss the following:

• Why is there joy in our longing and search for Jesus?

• What gifts can we bring Jesus?

• How is sacrificial living, or sacrificial giving, important to our discipleship?

Following this time of reading and discussion, invite each of the youth to write one thing that he or she would like to give Jesus in the coming year. (This could be a commitment of time, talent or treasure, or an act of service.)

Close in prayer.

SWEET CHRISTMAS

Supplies: Bible, markerboard, marker, Christmas cookie or piece of candy for each person

This brief icebreaker and devotional is a great way to open a group meeting. Give each participant a piece of candy or a Christmas cookie as he or she enters. After asking everyone to eat the candy, use a markerboard to record responses to the following question:

• Why, do you think, do we like sweets so much?

Following responses, read aloud **James 1:17,** which says, "Every generous act of giving, with every perfect gift, is from above."

Gather the youth into a circle, and say: "Several centuries ago a theologian named Saint Augustine said, 'We are restless until we find our rest in God.' " Ask:

• What, do you think, are some of God's greatest and sweetest gifts?

• In what ways are God's gifts lasting, rather than temporary?

• How can the Christmas season help us remember God's gifts?

Read aloud **James 1:17** again as a closing prayer.

BLUE CHRISTMAS

Many people suffer from depression, loneliness, or feelings of isolation during the Christmas season. The same can be true of teenagers. Children of divorce, students who struggle in school, and teens who have trouble making friends can all have difficulties during this season.

If you are looking for a way to encourage these teenagers, try handing or sending them (by text message, e-mail, or other means) some of these encouraging Scriptures and thoughts. This little devotional tool can make a difference to those youth who are struggling with seasonal anxiety or depression. This is an effective way for a youth minister, Sunday school teacher, or adult counselor to make a connection with teens who are struggling. You might also include your phone number as a reminder that they have someone whom they can call on.

Christmas is a season when we remember Emmanuel—"God is with us." And if God is with us, who can be against us?

I just want you to know that I am praying for you, and I want to encourage you during this season of God's love. May the peace of Christ be with you always!

DEPRESSED? Read **Psalm 30; Matthew 11:28-30.**

DISCOURAGED? Read **Habakkuk 1:1-3; 2:2-3; 1 John 5:1-5.**

HAVE AN ADDICTION? Read **Romans 7:14-25; 1 Corinthians 6:12-20.**

LONELY? Read **Psalm 68:1-10; Psalm 137:1-6; Psalm 139:1-18.**

THE TWELVE DAYS OF CHRISTMAS

Preparation: Send each of the tasks below to your youth by text message, mail, or e-mail or post them on the Web.

Many adults and youth do not realize that the twelve days of Christmas that we sing about in the popular tune are actually the twelve days between Christmas Day and the Epiphany (the day on which we celebrate the visit of the wise men). The list below gives the youth a way to celebrate each of the twelve days of Christmas.

Send each day's task to your youth as a text message, e-mail it, or post in on your youth ministry website or on a social networking site that many of your youth use. Challenge the youth to use the twelve days of Christmas to serve others, grow in their faith, and embody Christ's love.

1ST DAY OF CHRISTMAS (CHRISTMAS DAY)

Call a friend and wish him or her and his or her family a merry Christmas.

2ND DAY OF CHRISTMAS

Read and reflect on **Matthew 1:18-25** as you eat breakfast.

3RD DAY OF CHRISTMAS

Write a letter or an e-mail to a family member or friend who lives far away.

4TH DAY OF CHRISTMAS

Make a top ten list of things you are thankful for.

5TH DAY OF CHRISTMAS

Call a friend and invite him or her to church or a youth meeting.

6TH DAY OF CHRISTMAS

Send a postcard or letter to a teacher, a coach, or an adult who has helped you in some way.

7TH DAY OF CHRISTMAS

Do something nice and unexpected for your parent(s).

8TH DAY OF CHRISTMAS

Serve food to someone who is hungry, call on a homebound older adult, or make a gift for someone in need.

9TH DAY OF CHRISTMAS

Read and reflect on **1 Corinthians 13** before you go to bed.

10TH DAY OF CHRISTMAS

Read the first chapter of a good book.

11TH DAY OF CHRISTMAS

Read and reflect on **Matthew 2:1-12** before you go to bed.

12TH DAY OF CHRISTMAS

Decide how you will serve others in the coming year.

JINGLE ALL THE WAY

Supplies: sleigh bells or another small noisemaker and two blindfolds

This is a fun Christmas-themed game that is also funny to watch.

Have the group form a large circle, then select two participants to be in the middle. Blindfold both. Give one of these two teens the bells.

The object of the game is as follows: The person with the bells will attempt to flee from the other blindfolded person. The teen holding the bells cannot speak but must ring the bell every time the other blindfolded teen says, "Jingle." The other teens, who form the circle, are the boundary within which the game is played and will gently keep both teens inside the circle until the person without the bells can tag the one with the bells. Those around the circle also serve as spotters, who will keep the teens from bumping into each other.

Keep track of the time. If, after thirty seconds, the person without the bells has not tagged the one with the bells, two other teens will replace the blindfolded teens.

PAPER ANGELS

Supplies: Bible, used wrapping paper and/or newspaper, a roll of masking tape for every three or four youth

This is an easy and fun activity that will help teenagers work together. Younger teens, especially, will like this one.

Divide the group into clusters of three or four, and give each cluster used wrapping paper and/or some newspapers and some masking tape. Challenge each cluster to create the best paper angel, either by:

1. using one of their own youth members as a stand-up model and covering that teen with paper; or

2. creating a paper sculpture of an angel on the floor or on a tabletop.

See which cluster can create the best angel. (Be sure to recycle the paper when you are finished with it.) Then ask a volunteer to read aloud **Luke 1:26-38.** Explain that the word *angel* literally means "messenger." Ask the youth to talk about the ways in which they experience God's messages. Then ask a youth to read aloud **Hebrews 13:1-2.** Invite the teens to talk about times when they may have encountered an angel, without having known it at the time.

YULE HOUSE OR MINE?

Preparation: Make arrangements for families in your congregation to host the youth for one course of a meal.

Supplies: small gifts for the host families

Here's a unique twist on the traditional "progressive dinner" theme that is popular during the Christmas season. Instead of asking teenagers and their families to open their homes for one course of a progressive meal (appetizer, main course, or dessert), arrange for four or five other families from the church to open their homes to the teenagers. Try to involve some older adults or retirees who would welcome having someone to talk to. (Keep in mind that many older adults suffer from depression or feelings of loss or isolation during the holidays.) As much as possible, have a variety of types of families and homes.

Arrange for each household to host a small group of teenagers for about twenty minutes each. During this time, the hosts should tell the youth about one of their Christmas traditions or a special Christmas memory.

The youth, for their part, should bring small gifts or tokens of love and friendship for their hosts.

This event, which celebrates the true joy of Christ's birth, doesn't take much time. And more than simply singing Christmas carols in the nursing home hallways or having a Christmas party at the church, teenagers will find that this type of intimate conversation and gift-giving is rewarding and educational.

Worthwhile Winter Breaks

After Christmas, there are still some good days of vacation that have potential for ministry: New Year's Day; Martin Luther King, Jr., Day; Presidents Day; and snow days all hold possibilities. Here are some events, outings, and games that can help you make the most of these one-day breaks.

THE NEW YEAR

Preparation: Plan a gathering on New Year's Eve.

Supplies: Bible, food, decorations, supplies for a service or activities

Years ago, Christians would often gather on New Year's Eve for "watch night" services. These watch night gatherings offered people an opportunity to reflect on the past year, to give thanks for life's blessings, and to anticipate and pray about what God would do in the year to come.

Although watch night services are not as common as they once were, youth leaders may find that teenagers are open to gathering for New Year's Eve parties or to participating in learning opportunities before heading back to school.

Consider hosting a game night or movie night on New Year's Eve. Make some time during this gathering for a New Year's devotion, such as the one on page 62.

NEW THINGS

Preparation: Gather your group on New Year's Eve or another day before they return to school from Christmas break.

Supplies: Bible, paper, pens or pencils

This brief study can be used as a New Year's Eve reflection or as a devotion before the youth return to school.

Say: "What is God up to these days? The same old, same old? Or is God doing a new thing? Let's see what the Bible has to say. You might be surprised to find that God is a God of the new. God is still creating. God is still working. God is still performing miracles in you."

Ask one volunteer to read aloud **Psalm 96:1-6** and another to read aloud **Isaiah 43:18-19.** Then ask:

➜ Why, do you think, is it important for human beings to strive for new ideas, new ways of doing things, and innovations?

➜ What do these Scriptures tell us about God and God's intentions for our lives?

Ask one volunteer to read aloud **Jeremiah 31:31-34** and another to read aloud **2 Corinthians 5:16-17.** Then ask:

➔ What does God's new covenant look like?

➔ How do Jesus' life, death, and resurrection give us a new way of understanding and relating to God?

➔ What new things might God do in the coming year?

Gather the group into a circle. Hand out paper and pencils or pens. Instruct each person to jot down a few things that he or she hopes God will do in his or her life in the coming year.

Then close by praying the following:

God of the new, we are glad that you are still creating and bringing all things into a new creation. We pray that you would use us, too. Continue to mold us each day more and more into the likeness of your son, Jesus. Amen.

AND JUSTICE FOR ALL

Preparation: Obtain an audio recording of the famous "I Have a Dream" speech of Dr. Martin Luther King, Jr., which he delivered on the steps of the Lincoln Memorial in Washington, D.C., on August 28, 1963. Dr. King's speeches are now readily available in most libraries and on the Internet. If you find a recording of the speech online, make sure that it has been placed there legally and that you have read and are following the terms of use.

Supplies: Bible, paper, pens or pencils

Invite your teens to listen to this speech and to make notes about the high points and the insights that resonate most with them. After listening to the speech, allow the youth to talk about the notes they made and discuss why this speech was such an important moment in American history.

Point out that Dr. King quoted from the Bible. Then ask a volunteer to read aloud **Micah 6:6-8,** while the other youth follow along.

Then ask:

➜ What is justice?

➜ What aspects of justice were the prophet Micah and Dr. King speaking about?

➜ In what ways are we still working for this justice in America? How is this justice different from the justice we hear about in court decisions, legal dramas, or political debates?

➜ How can we be involved in making our community and nation more just?

Close with a prayer for the nation, for our leaders, and for the day that justice for all will be realized.

MARTIN LUTHER KING, JR., DAY

Preparation: Obtain excerpts from the speeches and/or writings of Dr. Martin Luther King, Jr.

Supplies: Bibles, excerpts from King's speeches and/or writings

Martin Luther King, Jr., Day is a day that affords youth the opportunity to reflect on issues of justice, inclusiveness, race, and minorities' continuing struggle for recognition and opportunity. Toward that end, here are two thought-provoking activities that can help teens reflect on biblical themes related to this important day.

FULFILLING THE DREAM

Beforehand, look for speeches and/or writings in which Dr. Martin Luther King, Jr., articulated his vision for the United States and the world. He is most famous for doing this in his "I Have a Dream" speech, which he delivered on the steps of the Lincoln Memorial on August 28, 1963. His other famous works include 1963's "Letter From Birmingham Jail" and 1968's "I've Been to the Mountaintop" speech, which he delivered the evening before his untimely death.

Bring in several pairs of prescription eyeglasses. You can gather these from youth and their parents or other members of your church, or purchase inexpensive over-the-counter reading glasses at a pharmacy or discount store.

After gathering your group, invite each teen to wear a pair of eyeglasses and to observe objects up close, at a distance, and far away. Have them jot down some of their observations and think about the following questions:

➜ What did the eyeglasses do to your vision?

➜ How did looking through the glasses help or hinder your ability to see clearly?

➜ How did looking through the various lenses "shock" you into seeing things in a new way?

Read aloud an excerpt from Dr. King's, speeches or writings. (See the description above.) Then read **Acts 2:14-21** together. Ask:

➜ What new vision for our world does this prophetic text describe?

➜ How is the "American dream" similar to or different from this vision?

➜ Through what "lenses" do we look at other people? Does our vision need correction?

➜ How, do you think, has Dr. King's vision for America been fulfilled? How has this vision remained unfulfilled?

Close with a prayer for the nation, for racial healing, and for the vision of God's holy and just kingdom to be realized.

PASS IT ON

Preparation: Prepare a message for your youth to pass along.

Depending on where in the country you grew up, you probably remember the excitement of a snow day, waiting by the television or the radio for the list of school closings.

No doubt, a snow day is one of the most wonderful gifts a teenager could ask for. If you know that most of your students are home on a snow day, make the most of the opportunity. Call two or three of your student leaders and give them some information, a Bible verse, or the date of an important upcoming youth event—and ask them to pass this information along to two or three others by calling them or sending text messages.

Be prepared for snow days by having a master list of your teenagers and their phone numbers). You may also ask your student leaders to call or text certain teens to make sure that the circle of information is completed. (Be sure to give them these phone numbers, too.)

SNOW ANGELS

Here's a fun snow day event that gets teenagers involved and connected, without having to leave home. Give your teenagers a call after school has been canceled. Ask each teenager to go outside and make a snow angel and to take a digital photo of his or her creation. Ask the youth to then share the pictures with the rest of the group on a social networking site, such as Facebook, or a photo-sharing site, such as Flickr. See which teenager can create the best snow angel.

SNOWBALLS

Preparation: Encourage your youth to store snowballs in their freezer.

Much like the Snow Angels event, send e-mails or text messages to your youth and invite them to make some snowballs and store them in their freezers at home.

Then later (say, in the middle of July) have the teenagers bring their snowballs to the youth group (in coolers) for a summer snow fest and snowball fight.

PRESIDENTS' DAY

Supplies: Bible

Many schools are out on the third Monday in February in celebration of Presidents' Day. Although most students enjoy simply having the day off, few give much thought to taking a day to honor or celebrate the office of the presidency. Presidents' Day is a great time for an outing or an afternoon at the movies. If you gather for such an activity, consider opening your time together with the following presidential devotion:

Invite a volunteer to read aloud **Romans 13:1-7.**

Divide the youth into groups of three or four, and have each group discuss any insights they gleaned from the biblical text. Allow each group to summarize its discussion.

Then, as an entire group, discuss the following questions:

➜ Why, do you think, does Paul ask us to obey the civil authorities?

➜ How is a government's authority similar to or different from God's authority?

➜ Do you think that a president of the United State is or can be God's servant? Why, or why not? How?

➜ When, in the history of the United States or another country, should people have *not* obeyed the authority of the president or other leader?

➜ In what ways can individual Christians and the church as a whole support a president of the United States?

➜ In what ways can the church speak truth to those in positions of authority?

➜ What specific challenges might a president face that would cause conflicts with his or her faith?

Spectacular Spring Break

Spring break has assumed cult-like status among many older teenagers. Every year, thousands of southbound students flock to beaches and sunny weather. Who can blame them? The arrival of spring break means liberation from months of sitting in the classroom.

But many youth, especially younger teens, stay home during spring break. For these youth, spring break offers superb opportunities for togetherness, service, and learning. Youth ministers may also find that spring break, much like the Christmas season, is a time when some youth are mired in isolation and loneliness. Meaningful church activities may give these youth something to look forward to while their peers are relaxing on the beach.

Other springtime breaks, such as Memorial Day weekend, also offer opportunities for ministry.

Try one or more of these refreshing springtime events to rejuvenate your youth.

STEPPING OUT

Preparation: Set up a spring break service project in your congregation or community.

If you were to ask your grandmother about "spring cleaning," she would no doubt have a few stories for you about dirty windows, hanging cobwebs, and dusty cupboards. If you want to help your youth engage in spring cleaning of a different sort, set up a spring break service project.

This project could involve visiting a soup kitchen in your community and both serving and sharing a meal with local persons who are hungry and/or homeless; doing yard work for older adults; or just heading out into the community and helping out wherever you spot a need.

You might also advertise in your church the availability of youth helpers. You'd be surprised at how many people, especially older adults, can use an extra hand. These intergenerational connections will also make your youth ministry more visible in your church.

GOD BE WITH YOU

Preparation: Photocopy the Spring Break Devotional, on pages 92-95, and give it to any youth who are leaving on spring break.

Invite your teens to use the devotional as they are traveling or as a study guide for each day of the break. Since the devotional is on two two-page spreads, you can easily photocopy it onto both sides of a single sheet of paper and fold it in half to make a handy four-page booklet. Or you could create an original devotional guide and customize it to your group. You might even invite youth or other members of the congregation to write devotionals.

Consider sending text messages to your youth during the break to remind them to set aside time each day for their Spring Break Devotional.

SPRING FLING

Preparation: Purchase a giant slingshot; and identify a large, open area outdoors. As you identify a space for your "Spring Fling," be sure that you are not too close to cars, windows, or other objects that could be damaged by high-velocity water balloons. Have access to a spigot so that youth can fill the water balloons.

Supplies: giant slingshot, several balloons

This fun game doesn't cost much or require much preparation. Some slingshots can toss a water balloon nearly the length of a football field, one hundred yards. These giant slings, which you can find pretty easily on the Internet or at many sporting goods stores, are a sure-fire way to get your young men involved. A lot of young women will enjoy them too.

Be clear that people should not be targets (unless you decide to put away the slingshot and have a good, old-fashioned water balloon fight).

SPRING CLEANING

Preparation: Photocopy the Spring Cleaning Devotional, on the last page of this book.

If you have an opportunity to meet with a group of your students during spring break, try this challenging study.

You will need Bibles and pens or pencils. Photocopy and distribute the Spring Cleaning Devotional on the last page of this book. (The text has been reproduced below.)

Read **Matthew 5:1-12.**

These brief teachings of Jesus are often called "The Beatitudes," which means "the beautiful teachings." Each beatitude is a little nugget of happiness that reveals a key to finding God through our actions and attitudes toward others. These teachings also challenge us and help us grow in our faith in God and love toward others.

As you read the Beatitudes again, write your responses to the following questions then discuss your answers with others in your group:

→ Which of these teachings is most relevant to you? Why?

→ Which is the most challenging for you? Why?

→ Which do you find the most comforting? Why?

→ Which of these do you find the most difficult to understand? How?

→ How might these beatitudes help us find happiness in life?

→ How do these teachings relate to our relationship with God? How do they relate to our relationships with others?

→ How could living by these teachings make our lives more meaningful?

As a group, pray aloud this prayer:

God of mercy, we want to be blessed. We want to discover the happiness that you offer. As we serve others, help us see that we are also serving you. When we love others, help us see that we also are loving you. And when we suffer, help us endure faithfully, even as Jesus endured the pain of the cross. Give us strength to live for you each day. Amen.

REMEMBER ME

Preparation: Ask the youth to submit names of friends who have died, along with the location of their graves. Be sure to check with the cemeteries you plan to visit about the kinds of decorations that are allowed.

Supplies: flowers, decorations, and/or other expressions of love and remembrance (such as signed letters)

Memorial Day presents some unique opportunities for youth. Originally called "Decoration Day," Memorial Day had its beginnings at the end of the Civil War, when people visited graves and decorated them to remember the battle fallen. Today, Memorial Day is always celebrated on the last Monday in May, and has taken on nuances of remembering not only those who have died in service to America but also family members and friends. Although the practice is not as popular as it was in past generations, many Americans still visit family graves sites to decorate the plots.

Memorial Day is a great opportunity for youth, as part of a Christian community, to remember the lives of friends, family members, and peers who have died.

A couple of weeks before Memorial Day, ask the youth to submit names of friends and family who have died and the locations of their graves. Then invite the youth to attend a cemetery visitation and remembrance on Memorial Day morning or at another time during the holiday weekend. Also ask youth to write letters to their deceased loved ones or to prepare cards featuring appropriate Bible verses (such as those listed below).

(continued on page 66)

Once you have gathered, drive to the grave sites (at least those that are local), taking along flowers, decorations, or other expressions of love and remembrance, as allowed by the cemetery. Invite the youth to leave behind their letters and cards along with the flowers and other decorations.

At each site, take a moment to reflect on the nature of friendship and love, pointing out the role of remembrance in our faith, as evidenced throughout the Bible, as well as the promise of resurrection. Some appropriate Bible passages to read aloud include the following:

➜ **Psalm 23** ("The LORD is my shepherd, I shall not want.")

➜ **1 Corinthians 15:50-58** ("For this perishable body must put on imperishability, and this mortal body must put on immortality.")

➜ **Philippians 1:3-11** ("I thank my God every time I remember you.")

➜ **Revelation 21:1-5** ("[God] will wipe every tear from their eyes. Death will be no more; mourning and crying and pain will be no more.")

78

Close your time at each grave site with a time of silence or selected prayers from the youth.

Option: If you cannot get a gathering of youth on Memorial Day, invite the teenagers to write thoughts or expressions of remembrance beforehand. A volunteer could take the notes to the cemetery and place them on the graves.

If appropriate, have your group sign a love note and send this to family members of the person who died, reminding them that you are praying for them in their loss.

Youth Leader Breaks and Renewal Adventures

One of the most important aspects of any ministry is rest and renewal. Those who don't take time or make time to recharge their own batteries will soon find that they have nothing left to give to others. It is a well-known fact that many youth leaders burn out in their first years of ministry. Others gravitate toward higher-paying ministry jobs or less-stressful pastures.

However, when it comes to youth ministry, a break for the students can be a break for the youth leader also. Adult leaders need refreshment. That is why every youth leader should schedule appropriate rest periods, vacations, and learning opportunities. Some of these can be most easily framed inside the school break.

Here you'll find ideas for expanding your mind and your heart. You'll also find some low-cost, unique ideas for recreation and rest. By scheduling a few of these into your calendar, you'll also find that you have more to give the teenagers you work with.

SOUL REST

Preparation: Find a location where you can spend time in retreat, and schedule a day to get away.

Every youth minister eventually needs (and deserves!) a break. This quiet experience can be a means of refreshing the spirit while also providing some deeper reflection.

First, schedule a day into your calendar (maybe a day during spring break, fall break, or the summer) when you can get away from the demands and obligations of your work, your family, and your personal pursuits. Find a monastery, a retreat center, or a campground that will allow you to stay overnight.

As you prepare to leave on your retreat, reflect on **Luke 9:1-6,** asking yourself the following questions:

→ Why did Jesus ask the disciples to travel light on their journey?

→ How has my life become encumbered by the weight of unnecessary possessions?

→ How might my ministry be revitalized through shedding some of these burdens?

→ What could I gain for my journey by not taking myself so seriously or by trusting more fully in God?

Obviously, this retreat should be light. Take along some favorite healthful foods, but forgo electronics—no television, no computer, no iPod. Take along a Bible and some other books that you would like to read. A good devotional guide would also be beneficial.

Allow this time to refresh your spirit and body. Take a nap. Take a walk. Reflect and pray. Talk to others at the retreat center or the monastery about your work and see what insights you might gain from the wisdom of others.

IF ONLY I HAD THE TIME

How often have you said to yourself: "I'd like to do such-and-such if only I had the time"? Use this brief exercise to develop a plan to embrace a new hobby, learn a new craft, see a beautiful sight, or travel to an exotic location.

First, complete the following three sentences. Don't worry if you have the same answer for all of them.

➔ The one thing I'd love to learn how to do is _____.

➔ I wish that I had time for _____.

➔ I wish that I could see _____.

After completing the sentences, you will likely find that a common theme or idea that is of paramount interest to you. Perhaps, you'd like to go down a river in a kayak, learn how to paint with watercolors, or see the Grand Canyon. Whatever it is, write down this activity, idea, trip, or project.

Then complete these sentences:

→ I have a free day on _____.

→ I will need a break after I _____.

→ The most promising time I will have available for a trip is _____

_____.

As you answer these questions, you will likely discover that there is a date or time that would work with your schedule. Write down this date, along with what you plan to do, and guard it.

Be sure to allow adequate time and planning for your special day or event.

TOUGH QUESTIONS

Church leaders need time and opportunities to ask and struggle with some tough questions. Over the years, I have taken many personal retreats (usually solo); and I've used these questions to challenge myself and guide my discernment process. I think that they will work well for you on a silent retreat or as a morning or evening reflection on your ministry.

PERSONAL QUESTIONS

➜ In what ways have I grown stale?

➜ What do I need most in my life right now?

➜ What or who are the sources of my greatest joy and pleasure?

➜ Where or how am I experiencing burnout, disinterest, or apathy in my life?

➜ What is the one thing I can do this week to improve my life and the lives of those in my family?

MINISTRY QUESTIONS

→ In what ways has my ministry or my commitment to serve God and others grown stale?

→ Where do I find the greatest sources of support and encouragement in ministry?

→ Where am I experiencing burnout, disinterest or apathy in my ministry?

→ What do I need most in my ministry right now?

→ What one thing can I do this week to make my ministry more effective or efficient?

THE REALLY TOUGH QUESTIONS

→ What sins in my life are holding me back from fully embracing God's will for my life?

→ In what ways do I need to trust God more?

→ Where am I demonstrating vulnerability, openness, and honesty in my walk with God?

→ With whom might I talk to help me grow spiritually?

→ What one change do I need to make in my life if I am to go to a deeper place with Christ?

REFLECTION

This personal retreat module, based on Mark's Gospel, can reap large rewards when used as a one-day session or a weekend getaway. Pray and reflect on the following Scriptures, using the questions below:

MARK 4:1-9 (THE PARABLE OF THE SOWER)

→ What does this parable teach me about ministry?

→ What does the parable tell me about the limitations of my ministry?

→ What does this parable say about my successes in ministry?

MARK 6:1-6 (JESUS IN HIS HOME TOWN)

→ In what ways does this story show the difficulties of ministry?

→ After reading this Scripture, where do I see myself in relationship to Jesus?

→ In what ways have people rejected my ministry?

→ In what ways have people accepted my ministry? Why?

MARK 9:33-41 (ARGUMENTS AND ANIMOSITIES)

→ How am I feeling about my service to others?

→ What stresses are accompanying me on this journey of service?

→ Why do I continue to do this work? What is motivating me?

→ What jealousies are complicating or hindering my ministry?

→ How can I give ministry away to others?

→ What rewards am I experiencing in this work?

MARK 10:46-52 (JESUS HEALS BARTIMAEUS)

➜ How has Jesus touched my life?

➜ Where do I need greater vision to see God's purposes and plans?

➜ What is empowering me to follow Jesus another day or year?

➜ Where has my heart grown faint?

➜ What is the most encouraging thing that I've seen God do this past year?

➜ Who is traveling alongside me in the work of youth ministry?

RE-CREATION

Sometimes youth leaders become so busy that they lose any incentive or ability to imagine the possibilities in their own lives. This can even be the case when we try to make time for refreshment. Here are fifty low-cost ideas that can be one-day re-creation opportunities.

→ Ride a bicycle.

→ Hike a trail.

→ Window shop.

→ Visit the library.

→ Listen to music.

→ Go fishing.

→ Knit or sew.

→ Call old friends.

→ Write letters.

88

- ➜ Read a Gospel.
- ➜ Paint a picture.
- ➜ Fingerpaint.
- ➜ Plant a garden.
- ➜ Plant a tree.
- ➜ Create a CD or playlist of your favorite songs.
- ➜ Write a song.
- ➜ Write poetry.
- ➜ Write a short story.
- ➜ Write about a memory.
- ➜ Count cars.

- ➜ Fast and pray.
- ➜ Go for a swim.
- ➜ Take a drive.
- ➜ Rent and row a kayak.
- ➜ Clean your closet.
- ➜ Buy new socks.
- ➜ Bake cookies.
- ➜ Sleep late.
- ➜ Visit a monastery.
- ➜ Sit in the airport and watch planes.
- ➜ People watch.
- ➜ Read a classic.
- ➜ Read a newspaper.
- ➜ Surf the Web.
- ➜ Scream in the woods.

- ➜ Visit a playground.
- ➜ Throw a Frisbee.
- ➜ Do yoga.
- ➜ Stretch and breathe.
- ➜ Balance your checkbook.
- ➜ Write a love note.
- ➜ Write and send thank-you notes.
- ➜ Cook soups.
- ➜ Watch a movie.
- ➜ Sit on the beach.
- ➜ Walk in the rain.
- ➜ Write and mail postcards.
- ➜ Spend time with family.
- ➜ Sip coffee or tea.
- ➜ Work on a scrapbook.

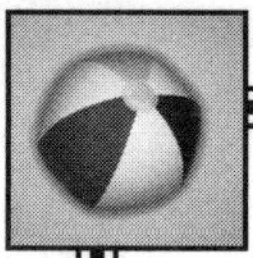

BREAK OUT—DAY 6

Memory Verse: Contribute to the needs of the saints; extend hospitality to strangers (**Romans 12:13**).

Reflect

➜ How am I contributing to my youth group? my church?

➜ Whom I could invite to our church or youth group?

Spring Forward

➜ Today I will give _____.

➜ I will invite _____ to church or youth group.

BREAK OUT—DAY 7

Memory Verse: Live in harmony with one another; do not be haughty, but associate with the lowly (**Romans 12:16**).

Reflect

➜ How do I show friendship to others?

➜ What attitudes do I need to adjust to be more like Jesus?

Spring Forward

➜ Today I will pray for _____.

➜ I will be a friend to _____.

SPRING BREAK DEVOTIONAL

BREAK OUT—DAY 1

Memory Verse: I appeal to you therefore, brothers and sisters, by the mercies of God, to present your bodies as a living sacrifice, holy and acceptable to God (**Romans 12:1**).

Reflect
➜ How am I glorifying God through my body?

➜ How can I give more of myself more fully to God?

Spring Forward
➜ Today I will pray for _____.

➜ I will dedicate myself to do_____.

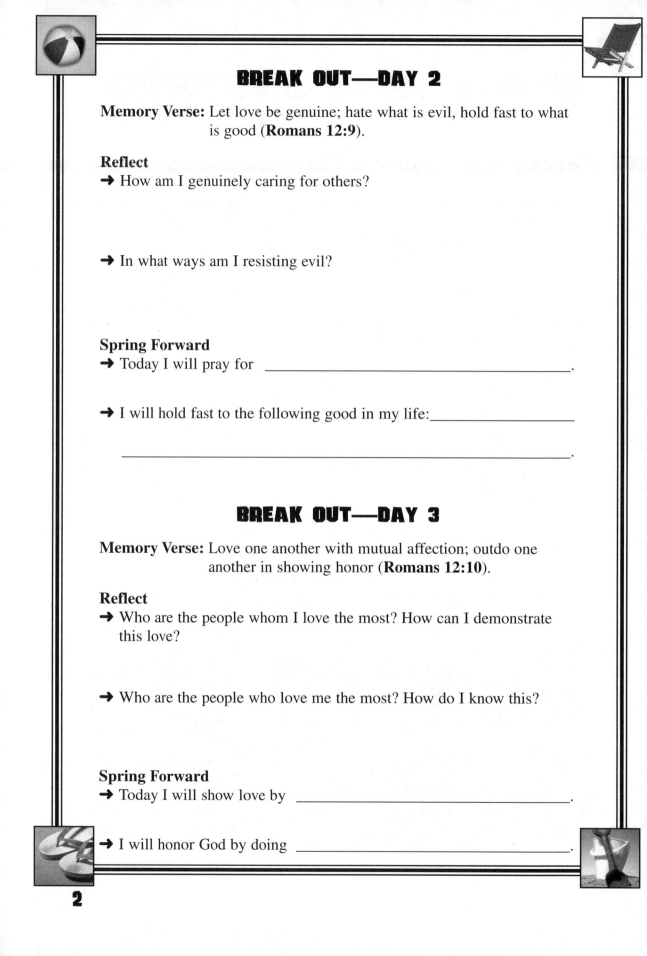

BREAK OUT—DAY 2

Memory Verse: Let love be genuine; hate what is evil, hold fast to what is good (**Romans 12:9**).

Reflect

➔ How am I genuinely caring for others?

➔ In what ways am I resisting evil?

Spring Forward

➔ Today I will pray for _____.

➔ I will hold fast to the following good in my life:_____

_____.

BREAK OUT—DAY 3

Memory Verse: Love one another with mutual affection; outdo one another in showing honor (**Romans 12:10**).

Reflect

➔ Who are the people whom I love the most? How can I demonstrate this love?

➔ Who are the people who love me the most? How do I know this?

Spring Forward

➔ Today I will show love by _____.

➔ I will honor God by doing _____.

BREAK OUT—DAY 4

Memory Verse: Do not lag in zeal, be ardent in spirit, serve the Lord (**Romans 12:11**).

Reflect
➜ What about my faith am I most passionate about?

➜ In what ways am I serving God?

Spring Forward
➜ Today I will serve God by _____.

➜ I will be zealous for_____.

BREAK OUT—DAY 5

Memory Verse: Rejoice in hope, be patient in suffering, persevere in prayer (**Romans 12:12**).

Reflect
➜ What gives me hope?

➜ How can I be more patient with others or in difficult situations?

Spring Forward
➜ Today I will pray for _____.

➜ I will give thanks for _____.

SPRING CLEANING DEVOTIONAL

Read **Matthew 5:1-12.**

These brief teachings of Jesus are often called "The Beatitudes," which means "the beautiful teachings." Each beatitude is a little nugget of happiness that reveals a key to finding God through our actions and attitudes toward others. These teachings also challenge us and help us grow in our faith in God and love toward others.

As you read the Beatitudes again, write your responses to the following questions then discuss your answers with others in your group:

→ Which of these teachings is most relevant to you? Why?

→ Which is the most challenging for you? Why?

→ Which do you find the most comforting? Why?

→ Which of these do you find the most difficult to understand? How?

→ How might these beatitudes help us find happiness in life?

→ How do these teachings relate to our relationship with God? How do they relate to our relationships with others?

→ How could living by these teachings make our lives more meaningful?

As a group, pray aloud this prayer:

God of mercy, we want to be blessed. We want to discover the happiness that you offer. As we serve others, help us see that we are also serving you. When we love others, help us see that we also are loving you. And when we suffer, help us endure faithfully, even as Jesus endured the pain of the cross. Give us strength to live for you each day. Amen.